BEGINNING AGAIN

Hazelden Titles of Related Interest

Choosing Happiness: The Art of Living Unconditionally, Veronica Ray

Worthy of Love: Meditations on Loving Ourselves and Others, Karen Casey

BEGINNING AGAIN

Beyond the End of Love

Meditations for Starting Over

Will Limón

A Hazelden Book
HarperCollins*Publishers*

FIRST HARPERCOLLINS PAPERBACK EDITION PUBLISHED IN 1992.

Library of Congress Cataloging-in-Publication Data

Limón, Will.
    Beginning again : meditations for starting over / Will Limón
        p.   cm.
    "A Hazelden book"
    ISBN 0–06–255312–7
    1. Separation, (Psychology)—Religious aspects—Meditations.   2. Bereavement—Religious aspects—Meditations.   3. Adjustment (Psychology)—Religious aspects—Meditations.
    I. Title
BV4905.2.L45   1992
155.9'37—dc20
                                        91–55292
                                             CIP

---

92 93 94 95 96 K.P. 10 9 8 7 6 5 4 3 2 1

Dedication

For Kate.

For all the participants of my divorce
adjustment seminars. I hope these pages
reflect your abundant courage
and compassion.

Acknowledgments

I have been influenced and inspired by many individuals. Chief among these are the hundreds of participants in the divorce adjustment seminars I have taught. Their courage and determination to prevail over their pain stand as a testament to the human spirit. To them I owe a great deal.

I express my deepest gratitude to my wife Kate for her love, patience, and encouragement. I extend my special appreciation to Dr. Bruce Fisher for his creation of the Fisher Divorce Adjustment Seminar and his long-time support; to Bob Hoffman for his loving friendship, steadfast confidence in my abilities, and down-to-earth celebration of life; and to Deb Robson for her advice and encouragement.

I also extend my heartfelt thanks to Judy Delaney, my editor at Hazelden Educational Materials, who enthusiastically championed this book through all the publication hurdles and provided thoughtful, sensitive, and necessary editing. I also thank Jeanne Engelmann for her editorial assistance. And finally, I thank my Higher Power for inspiration, guidance, and strength.

INTRODUCTION

This book is about change. To be sure, each one of us faces change daily in many ways. From small disappointment to major inconvenience to tragedy, every change is born from some kind of loss. Even when change is positive, the hidden losses of former habits, attitudes, and relationships create subtle discomfort in our world: a discomfort we must adjust to.

Few changes are as life-altering as the loss of a significant love relationship through separation or divorce. As our relationship with a person ends, so end many of our hopes and dreams, as well as our view of ourselves in the world. To begin again after such a loss often seems an insurmountable task. Just rising and functioning from one day to the next may appear impossible. Many of us feel depression, rage, and hopelessness as we confront our ever-pressing daily routines. We're especially susceptible to stress-related physical illness as well as alcohol and other drug abuse.

Yet, with each ending comes room for another beginning. Whether we realize it or not, we choose from within what our lives are to be each day, each hour, *each thought*. Beginning again is realizing that choice. Beginning again is grieving and feeling anger through this loss, honoring the relationship, and letting go of it so we may continue to live. Beginning again is seeing the promise in the pain and our growth through this change.

Someone said, "Nothing is more certain than change." Life *is* change. To learn the sorrow and serenity inherent in experiencing change to the fullest is to realize the joy of living. "One choice at a time. One change at a time and one day at a time," writes Sharon Wegscheider-Cruse, concerning the path of the recovering alcoholic or adult child of an alcoholic. This makes good sense for all of us, including those of us whose changes come from the painful loss of a love.

I hope these meditations and affirmations will give you an anchor while you live through these painful days, and inspire you to make this a time of greater understanding and growth. The meditations will guide you through the recovery process. You may begin reading at any place in the book, but you will understand the process best by starting from the beginning.

"That which does not kill me makes me stronger," wrote the philosopher Nietzsche. We get stronger when we face losses and change with the willingness to truly live.

BEGINNING AGAIN

None are so blind as those who will not see.
    – Unknown

I Have No Denial

Life is good. Things are great. Except for a sensation like having a large hole in my chest, I'm fine. Oh, I have trouble sleeping, and my head keeps aching. Sometimes I hardly eat at all, while other days I stuff myself. Often I have trouble concentrating, and it's all I can do to drive safely across town. But, except for these complaints, and occasional outbursts of anger or a sudden surge of tears for no apparent reason, I'm doing all right.

Who am I fooling? I've never had so many things wrong with me for "no apparent reason." Something is not right. When I'm honest with myself, I see some real problems. My love-relationship has ended. I didn't plan on this, and now I'm not sure what to do. My friends try to console me when they say, "Time heals all wounds." They tell me to put a smile on my face and I'll soon be over it. I hope they're right, but I don't believe time or wishful thinking will take care of my symptoms.

I will stop denying my feelings and admit my pain. I know my pain won't disappear by ignoring it. Instead, I will help myself heal by letting myself feel it.

Today, I accept my pain so I may heal from it. It's a relief to stop denying that I hurt.

– ❈ –

Being human is difficult. Becoming human is a lifelong process. To be truly human is a gift.
– Abraham Heschel

The Never-Ending Journey

Just as I cannot see the beginning of my life, so the end remains a mystery. I spend my hours on the journey between these two awesome points in time. While I wish I were a whole person free from pain and finished with my personal growth, God is never finished with me. The end of my relationship is just another part of my journey.

The strength of my character is not built during the easy, happy times. It is forged in the fire of facing life as it is, especially in painful periods. Just as my body creates more muscle to meet the demands of physical labor, so my mind, heart, and soul expands as I confront my problems.

I must live with the reality of this loss, feel the hurt, experience the anger, and wrestle with the loneliness. Growing from this part of the journey is the promise in the pain. This is also a great challenge, and it is the path I must follow.

Today, I experience my loss as a challenge to be met. I grow from my pain.

— ❋ —

That which does not kill me makes me stronger.
— Friedrich Nietzsche

To Feel My Sorrow

Today, I will feel my sadness, the heaviness within my chest, the hurt within my heart, and the tightness around my throat. I will feel it through to cleanse myself of the pain.

I will find a time and place for solitude. There, I will listen to my body as I would to my best friend, and I will let my tears rise and flow like waves upon the sand. I will not be ashamed and I will not drown. I will simply be with my sorrow through this time.

As I speak the words of hurt, I'll feel the loss of my loved one and the holes left in my life, love, and future. And, I will mourn.

I feel my sadness, and it cleanses me of
this pain. With each moment of grief,
my burdens are being released.

— ❄ —

When a man takes one step toward God, God takes more steps toward that man than there are sands in the worlds of time.
— The Work of the Chariot

Who Is With Me in My Hurt?

I feel abandoned. My loved one has left me. Others appear preoccupied with their own loves and lives, while I have only emptiness and pain. Though I pray, my hurt is so deep and my impatience so great, I even drown out the messages of God. I begin to believe no one wants me, so I start to pull away from life itself.

Though this ending was not my doing, this isolation is. I will reach out to others and allow them to support me. We are here to be together. And though we all suffer losses, we have not lost everything. In our common misfortunes and shared sorrows, our burdens become lighter and life becomes more precious.

Today, I am not alone. I let God and my fellow human beings know that I hurt, and I accept their support.

— ❋ —

It was on my fifth birthday that Papa put his hand on my shoulder and said, "Remember, my son, if you ever need a helping hand, you'll find one at the end of your arm."

– Sam Levenson

Following My Inner Child

The greatest pain I feel comes from my inner child. This beautiful, innocent being from whom I've grown lives within me and still seeks the dreams of youth, yearns for the joy of a promised life, needs the stroking hand of love. Wrapped inside all my other pain, this part of me sees my loss as yet another betrayal of a grown-up world.

I can find energy in the innocence of my inner child. Just as small children have fun with simple objects and change quickly from tears to smiles, so I can learn resiliency to help me cope with life as it is now.

The task of my grown-up self is to learn from my loss. My entire being must experience my feelings. Yet, I find the sunlight after this storm only by listening to my inner child and following its dreams.

Today, I follow my inner child, listen to its simple wants, satisfy its needs, and use its energy to live.

— ❄ —

Let me tell thee, time is a very precious
gift of God; so precious that it's only given
to us moment by moment.
– Amelia Barr

The Time of My Life

I watch time. It moves slowly, marking the seconds, minutes, and hours of my sleepless nights. I wish it would either pass with the speed it had before my loss or stop altogether and suspend everything, including my pain, so I could settle into a gray numbness.

I must remember, though, that each unit of time, the moment that lasts or the hour that flies, is my life. Its varied pace is only my perception. And though time may seem to travel at a speed I do not like, it always moves evenly. I will learn to live within the natural pace of time, and seek to value each moment. This minute is mine to make the most of – and this minute is all I ever really have.

As I live my life today, I accept the constant rhythm of time. I concentrate on the best way to use the time I have.

– ❋ –

When patterns are broken, new worlds emerge.
– Tuli Kupferberg

Cutting Heartstrings

Though my loved one's gone, I sometimes find that I still hold our union in my heart. It glows there like an ember from a dying fire. Each time I try to leave, I draw back to its fading warmth because I hope somehow to rekindle this flame.

My efforts here are useless. They only add further sorrow, greater anger, and more abandonment. But these feelings are not the problem. It's the belief that I can make my love return that maintains my constant hurt. It's way past time for me to believe the truth: This love is over and lives only in my memory. Its absence is not just today, but forever. I must accept this today and in the future. By cutting the heartstrings that bind me to my love, I'll free myself.

By letting go of this love, I release the painful past, I heal from my anguish, and I liberate myself.

I let go of this love and free myself.

– ❄ –

Sometimes I go about pitying myself,
and all the time I am being carried on
great winds across the sky.

– Ojibway

When I Think Life's
Not Worth Living

There are days so exhausting that the stress of going on seems overwhelming. And there are those interminable nights when the pain inside me feels so great I think I may burst.

During these times I must stop pitying myself and sense the abundant energy all around me. The strength of nature shows itself each day if I choose to perceive it. Loved ones and friends are close by if I choose to reach out. The energy I need is everywhere.

I must admit to myself that I can't get through this alone, that I need to reach out to others for help and receive their shared strength. I will find energy when I quiet all my thoughts and listen for the simple

messages of my Higher Power. From these,
I draw new vitality to live.

*I ask for help from others and from my
Higher Power. I accept their love.*

– ❄ –

Dedicated in loving memory to Guy L.

I shall tell you a great secret, my friend.
Do not wait for the last judgment.
It takes place every day.
– Albert Camus

The Anger in My Heart

I entered my love-relationship for the joy
I would find in it. Now I realize that I
wanted more than I received. I am angry
about some things that were done and said,
and about others that were left undone or
unspoken. I am as angry about the complications of my present life as about the loss
of my relationship.

This anger creates an energy in me that I
must deal with. I can channel this energy
to improve my life: Increasing effort in my
career, taking the risk of making new
friends, learning new ways of having fun.

I know this anger shows I invested in my
relationship. But I want neither bitterness
nor depression, so I am willing to express
anger and guide its energy.

I accept my anger. I express it in healthy ways
that let my heart open up once again.

– ❆ –

The only thing we have to fear is fear itself.
– Franklin Delano Roosevelt

I Am Afraid

I feel overwhelmed by my loss and the changes it brings, the emotional turmoil, the eerie emptiness. I have so many doubts that I hide in the corners of life. I question whether there's anything left but fear. The answer is that life is still here, but I will not see it while I stay wrapped in anxiety and fright.

I wonder if my fear is based on reality, or if it comes from what I *expect* to happen. Fear is the result of unfounded expectations about the future. As my despair paralyzes me, the gloom I feel comes not from reality, but from the fear that the future may be more than I can bear.

How do I need to change? I can stop defining the future by the present. I'll reduce this fear by living with what comes in each new day. Though it has been a struggle, I will move on with my life and stop feeding my fears.

I live in today and stop dwelling on thoughts of a fearful future.

– ❁ –

...and our very anger said a new "Yes" to life.
– Betty Friedan

The Power of Grief and Anger

Sometimes I'm caught between my grief and my anger. These emotions affect me at the deepest level. I must accept that they're both a part of me. And though extremely painful, their combination signals greater strength than I've ever known. This strength is my energy to live.

I would not have such hurt if I had not loved so deeply. This anger wouldn't be so forceful if I had not felt so betrayed. These feelings show my investment not only in this relationship, but in life. So, I will cry my tears, feel my anger, and experience the emotions that give my life color. At times I may think that I'm going crazy when I do this, but to hold them back would be true insanity.

The anger I experience along with my grief shows me that my life matters. I will use this energy to launch me into my future.

Grief and anger give me power to heal.
I use this to move into a new life.

— ❋ —

*Happiness is experienced when your life
gives you what you are willing to accept.*
– Ken Keyes

Acceptance

I've fought against this loss and all that
comes with it. Often, I created fantasies of
how my life could have been, should have
been, or may yet become. I have run away
from reality and this kept me from starting
to heal.

How much of my current pain comes
from a struggle to change the unchange-
able? I may not like the truth. I may not
want this situation. But just as I can't stop
rain from falling, so this fighting only
leaves me exhausted from wasted effort.
What would happen if I used the same
amount of energy to accept reality?

As I learn to accept what is, I can stop
trying to control the uncontrollable. Also, I
can see more clearly what is manageable –
my response to the changes in my world.

*I accept my loss and the world as it is. I channel
my desire for change into changing myself.*

– ❊ –

*Courage is not the absence of fear.
It is the mastery of it.*
– S. N. Behrman

I Am Strong

My loss has changed my life, and I'm trying to understand the world from this new perspective. I have often felt weak, damaged, nearly destroyed. Yet, underneath it all, I find the courage and strength I need.

I have the courage to rise each day and face the sun without my loved one. I have the strength to do the work in my life. Memories flood my mind until I think I may lose it, but I don't. I am strong and I simply carry on. Even as I cry over the loss of the life I had planned, I am strong, for only the very strong can feel pain and keep on going.

I do not ignore the courage this requires. Though my loss felt like an ending, I will endure. With each new day I am healing.

In my daily living, my courage gives me strength to recover from my loss.

– ❋ –

*We are not troubled by things, but by the
opinion which we have of things.*
– Epictetus

Overcoming Loneliness

I'm aware of being alone. I often feel
isolated, lonely, and abandoned. I am so
accustomed to feeling lost that I fear I may
never be found.

I want to connect with someone, yet I am
paralyzed by fear that I will reach out and
find no one there. With the end of my love-
relationship, I fear I may have lost my only
link to the fulfillment I desire.

As I look into my inner mirror, at first I
see only myself. Exploring further, I find
my parents and family, my friends, and I
remember my love. I am flooded with
memories. Then, deep inside, I realize that
I am still connected to many people and
these connections to others will help me
overcome my loneliness.

*I view loneliness as temporary, not permanent.
I remember my relationships with others.*

– ❄ –

*The greatest discovery of my generation is
that man can alter his life simply by altering
his attitude of mind.*

– William James

As I Believe

I understand everything through the
filter of my beliefs. If I fear storms, hearing
wind can encourage fear in what I think
and feel, even if no storm approaches. In
this way, everything I perceive triggers
reactions based on what I value or believe.

Losing this relationship has shaken my
reality, as I now question just what it is I do
believe. A lesson in this loss is that it gives
me space to find anew who I will be. I
know that this is part of life, and I believe it
will bring me better things. When I accept
positive messages in my life, I realize my
power to renew myself.

*I believe in life, its lessons and its wisdom.
I am open to what this time teaches me.*

— ❈ —

Indeed we are running away all the time to
avoid coming face to face with ourselves.
– Anonymous

When I Feel I Will Explode

There are those days when living is a volatile mixture, and life is full of sparks to set it off. I explode at everything and everyone, including myself. I never wanted this loss, and I'm angry! I scream with rage, slowly seethe inside, or burn my friends with acrid, "teasing" jokes that melt the bonds I have with them. My life feels out of control and my body begins to break from all this stress.

I can understand this: We often feel angry when really we are hurt, fearful, or frustrated from not getting what we want. I can let my anger teach me about myself and learn to harness its energy to forge new directions.

I discover what is behind my anger. I contain and
channel the energy of my anger toward attitudes
and behavior that help me heal.

– ❋ –

*You will suffer and you will hurt. You will
have joy and you will have peace.*
– Alison Cheek

The Value of Grief

I remove the barriers to my sadness.
And, as I allow this grief to flood my being,
it wraps around me and holds me tenderly.
Though I've tried to avoid this sadness
through distractions or anger, I now find
this gentle sorrow to be a surprising relief.

I express my grief. And as I do, tears
wash the poisons from my heart. They
soften and calm me like a day of misting
rain cools and renews the earth. This
sorrow heals, for this is the value of grief:
When I allow my sadness to be real, I go
through it into the radiance of my future.
Slowly, silently, I heal.

*Today, I experience my grief and heal
through the comfort of this sorrow.*

— ❖ —

If I trim myself to suit others
I will soon whittle myself away.

– Anonymous

When I Believe
No One Wants Me

When I don't feel accepted or loved, the rejection I suffer is often overpowering. No matter how this happened, it was not what I wanted. Sometimes I even believe it wouldn't have occurred if I were truly desirable.

Let me be honest as I dwell on this. I must understand that this was an involvement with one other person on this planet, no less and no more. Though this connection may be severed, not all bonds to life are cut. I need not give away the world to mourn this single love.

Perhaps I gave too much. I did not mean to relinquish my identity by surrendering myself to this relationship. Yet, my feelings of rejection teach me that I did this very thing. Sacrificing my identity for someone else does not leave anything for me.

Healthy connections to another start with self-love, for it is up to me to embrace and nurture myself. In this way I can always be whole.

My feelings of rejection teach me to invest in myself. I will always have myself.

— ❋ —

God has entrusted me with myself.
– Epictetus

My Life, My Choice

I am experiencing much pain and frustration from the effect my partner's actions have had on my life and my dreams. I feel powerless to alter these emotions.

But, I forget what I can do for myself. Each day, I have countless choices for my thoughts, feelings, and actions. While my impact on people and events is limited, I always have the power to find the best or the worst in what happens. I must never forget, regardless of what others may do, that this is *my* life and *my* choice.

Each day I can consciously choose my life: My thoughts, my feelings, and my behavior. Today, I am thankful the choices are mine and no one else's.

Today, I choose my responses to life.

– ❄ –

Victory is won not in miles, but in inches.
Win a little now, hold your ground, and
later win a little more.

– Louis L'Amour

When I Want It All Right Now

I live in an impatient society. We have
instant coffee, microwave dinners, and
countless fast-relief medications. It's easy
for me to get caught up in this "instant-
ness." So I wonder, why can't my recovery
happen just as fast?

Recovery takes time. As my relationship
developed over time, so its ending was also
gradual, not as sudden as I think. I deceive
myself when I believe that healing should
be swift. What looks like sudden progress
in this world is almost always a break-
through built on many hours of painstaking
effort. My recovery will come with
thoughtful, consistent work.

I may want to be healed right now, but
health will come to me sigh by sigh, tear by
tear, smile by smile. As the saying goes,
"Small steps make a distance."

Today, I use my energy to heal
as patiently as I can.

– ❊ –

*He who knows others is wise. He who
knows himself is enlightened.*

– Lao-tzu

Intimacy

It seems like a lifetime since I was truly
close to another human being. With some
people I share my thoughts, with others my
feelings, but since my loss I haven't shared
full intimacy with anyone. I miss this more
than anything else.

Though I feel the absence of this special
bond I do not want to become intimate
with anyone just yet. I need to explore who
I am in relation to myself, rather than to
others. As I grow and change, I want to
understand and nurture this new self.

I need this time to know myself. If I start
relating closely with others too soon, it may
slow my growth. I won't wait forever, but
for now, to be patient and heal while
sharing some of myself with my friends,
give me what is best.

*I am just where I need to be. I celebrate
my new growth by recognizing it within.
I am intimate with myself.*

– ❀ –

Some people talk about finding God —
as if He could get lost.
– Anonymous

I Am Not Alone

There are days when I can connect with no one. All the faces I see appear strange, unknown, and incapable of knowing me. I seem surrounded by an invisible barrier that divides me from the world, and I suffer in the awful silence of confinement. It is easy to sink into these days, so easy that they could stretch to weeks or months or longer.

But I am not lost or forgotten. Though I am not always aware of God's presence, God is aware of me. How else would I be able to make it through each day? Where else would I find the strength to continue? My Higher Power is always with me, around me, in me.

Now that I know I am not alone, I look to this partnership to help me heal.

Today, I stay connected to life by being
conscious of my Higher Power.

– ❋ –

Life may be hard, but it's also wonderful.
– Small Change (movie)

Everything Is a Gift

From time to time, through this emotional fog, I become aware of things other than my lost relationship. I see the sun rise. I hear traffic, people talking, other sounds of living. Out there trees still stand, flowers still bloom, and seasons still pass. I realize that what is shattering to me doesn't seem to faze this world. How does life go on?

There is comfort in this wondering. I notice the shape of a cloud, the color of a flower petal, the scent in the air after a rain – soft, clean, almost sensual. Color, sound, sight, and smell flood my senses, telling me these are gifts from God that make my life worthwhile. Living is like a gift we open without knowing what will be inside. While I may not like all that I find, the difficult, painful parts teach me more than all the rest combined.

I give thanks for all of my life – both the joyous parts and the hurtful.

– ❄ –

*In the depths of winter, I finally learned that
within me there lay an invincible summer.*
– Albert Camus

The Rebirth in Me

I come to learn that there is no birth
without death. Though I wish to cast my
eyes away from my loss, I understand the
bittersweet message that nothing lasts
forever, that what makes something
valuable is its limited span of time.

From the cycle of the seasons, I come to
understand that death brings rebirth–that
it begins another change. So I see myself
within this rhythm of change, with death
and birth as partners. This happens each
time I let go of my love-relationship and
feel the pain of loss in balance with the
relief of release.

The death in me, this death, is part of life.
While this loss leaves a hole in who I am,
it also leaves a space to be filled. As I have
dealt with many kinds of loss in the past,
I will renew. I know that winter's chill
brings summer's warmth.

*On this day, I see through the death in me
to find new life. I am reborn.*

– ❋ –

Since everything is but an apparition, perfect
in being what it is, having nothing to do with
good or bad, acceptance or rejection,
one may well burst out in laughter.

– Long Chen Pa

Am I Having Fun Yet?

Though perhaps hidden, there is a person inside me who wants to have fun, an inner child who knows the joys of living. Even in dark moments, my inner child may smile and tease and help me see a bit of humor.

From these times of brief sunlight, when I laugh out loud and wonder at the sound, I realize my life must include this humor. Laughter of the soul as well as the body can bring relief from the constant heaviness. Like the child who thrills to the roller coaster ride without analyzing it, I can feel giddy from all the change in my life.

Fun is good medicine; humor is like salve on a wound. Humor and fun can help me keep my life in perspective and return my equilibrium.

I let my inner child have fun again.
I find balance by being with people
who remind me of the joys of living.

– ❊ –

*Happy are those who dream dreams and are ready
to pay the price to make them come true.*
– L. J. Cardinal Suenens

I Will Do What It Takes

For far too long, I've wished my life was different. I've dreamed of better things, a happier day, a satisfying future. Then, I awoke and nothing had changed.

I must realize that I create my future by what I am able and willing to do. So, for my future to hold the happiness I desire, I must be willing to do not only what is comfortable, but also what is necessary regardless of the discomfort, risks, and pain.

I prolong my agony when I avoid the tears of grief, the energy of anger, and the fear of my loneliness. If I don't face reality, I will keep myself from what I truly desire – the serenity of healing. There is no substitute for doing what it takes to heal.

*Today, I dedicate myself to my healing process
and do what is necessary.*

– ❊ –

Those things that hurt, instruct.
– Ben Franklin

Living With My Pain

Each day provides its special challenges, but none so great as seeing what is really there. I've found a thousand ways to hide from reality, but my pain remains. So today I won't shrink from my pain. Instead, I will live with it.

By seeing life completely, I can find hope. I can become aware of what I have, not just what's missing. I can appreciate what is positive in the present, and I can bring that into the future. By being realistic, I regain the energy I was using to hide from my pain. Only from this reality can I begin to heal.

I accept my life as it is.
I heal as I see life realistically.

– ❄ –

We grow toward the light, not toward darkness.
– Ashley Montagu

I Am Alive

Just for today, let me look at nature and realize I am alive. As flowers bloom, as trees regain leaves, as birds soar through the air and all fulfill their purpose in life, so I too have a place on this planet for living, sharing, and loving.

Just for today, let me banish the negative beliefs that dampen my love of life. Instead, I will become as quiet as the deepest forest. Then, as I observe the endless harmony of nature, I will feel a renewed flow of life.

Today, I will just be and accept life. I know I am alive, and as surely as there is life, I am well.

I release my negative thoughts and accept all that is within me as part of being alive.

— ❄ —

The highest reward for man's toil is not what he gets for it, but what he becomes by it.
– John Ruskin

I Can Forgive

Because of what has happened to me, it is hard to forgive. The hurt and anger I have toward my loved one, myself, the whole world, even my Higher Power, impairs my ability to forgive. Sometimes I believe life consists only of anger and hurt and unhappiness. When I think this, I tear open wounds and will not let them heal.

I must forgive and I can forgive. Forgiving does not mean that what happened is suddenly all right, or that my loss does not matter. But I can only hold so much bad feeling inside. Rather, forgiving is a release, so I may become who I will be.

I must forgive and I will. I will feel my emotions through and be healed. Honestly forgiving will help me become a person who can once again experience the joy and beauty of life.

I forgive. As I let go, I heal and become a new person.

– ❋ –

*Most folks are about as happy as they
make up their minds to be.*
– Abraham Lincoln

I Am Who I Aim to Be

I didn't wish for this to happen. How
can I be happy when what I have is not
what I want?

It's no secret that what we strive for helps
form our experiences. Am I seeking self-
acceptance, well-being, serenity? Mostly
I've sought to rid myself of pain. Then, I
find my actions only lead to continued hurt
and unhappiness because I've already
decided I can't be happy without my loved
one.

Maybe it's time to decide differently.
Maybe it's time to choose happiness even
though I often feel hurt, anger, and emptiness. Since this is my choice, I may as well
choose what I want. If I become who I aim
to be, I will aim for being a happy person.

*Today, I decide to be a happy person.
I celebrate my emerging self.*

– ❈ –

As you think, you travel, and as you love, you attract. You are today where your thoughts have brought you; you will be tomorrow where your thoughts take you.

– James Allen

Loving Myself

Sometimes I think that because I lost the person I loved, I've lost all love. Instead, I can remember that I was able to give love and I was loved in return. Now I realize that the love I had for that other person can be a gift I give to myself.

By loving myself, I turn toward myself the feelings of love that I've long desired to give another. This self-love helps me love others and makes me more receptive to another's love. In doing this, I understand that loving and being loved begin with me.

Today, I direct my love-flow toward myself. I give to myself what I desire to bestow on others.

– ❈ –

Life can only be understood backwards, but it must be lived forward.

– Søren Kierkegaard

I Will See This Through

I'm amazed at how time can be relative to how I feel. An afternoon of pleasure flies by. Yet an hour I spend in pain drags on. While I live through both, the pain always seems to last far longer. But, I will see both experiences through.

As much as I might wish for it, my life is not filled with joy all the time. Right now, my life often feels filled with hurt and anger. Yet strangely, this creates an intensity of living, much as a burn or scrape lets me know my skin exists.

Just as my skin takes its time to heal, so I must be patient with my emotional wound. To heal, as to live, takes the willingness to live through difficult times and accept both pain and its lessons. In this way, I do more than return to health. I grow beyond who I was before.

As I accept and grow through this painful time, I become more than I have ever been before.

– ❋ –

No matter where you go, there you are.
– Earnie Larsen

Finding My Peace

Throughout this turmoil, I yearn for peace in my life. Often I believed a job or a relationship or a place to live would bring me serenity. Now, as life continues to feel upside-down, it appears that nothing can bring me the peace I desire.

I keep forgetting that my peace is just that, *my* peace. Other people or material possessions may contribute to my sense of well being, but they don't make me well, whole, or serene. The more I seek outside of me, the less I search inside for what I can give to myself. And though others may, by words and actions, lead me to discover more about who I am, it is only when I look for peace inside myself that I understand what their messages mean.

The peace I seek dwells within me at all times.
I choose to find it.

– ❄ –

*There ain't no cloud so thick that the sun
ain't shinin' on t'other side.*

– Rattlesnake, an 1870s mountain man

What I Worry For

Though in other times I've worried, I feel
now like worry itself, so often does it color
my every thought and action. Because my
world has been ripped open, I fear my
whole life may flow away.

What is this worry? It is fear that what
happened will continue to affect my life.
As I define the future by what is in the
present, this fear springs from my sense of
powerlessness and my belief that I might
feel powerless forever. I'm worried about
losing *me*.

As I begin to heal and find new strength
in transforming from survival to growth, I
can let go of my worries. The past need not
frighten me. Nurturing a partnership with
my Higher Power gives me the energy to
make my future greater than I've ever
imagined.

My partnership with God helps me grow.

— ❊ —

*Loneliness is a word to express
the pain of being alone.
Solitude is a word to express
the glory of being alone.*
– Paul Tillich

Being Alone

In a certain sense, I am alone throughout my life. No one knows my joy and hurt as I do. This does not mean I am by myself, however. While I am always an individual, I am always part of a whole. When I feel lonely, it is important to realize that *feeling* lost doesn't mean *being* lost.

There are two lessons to be learned from aloneness. First, I can use solitude to help me learn who I am. During these times, I have a quiet space to feel all there is within me, without the distraction of the outside world. These are times to refresh myself. Second, I can take this opportunity to understand my need for intimacy with others, since my loneliness is really a hunger for relationships.

The better I understand myself and my needs, the closer I am to getting my needs met. Because of this, I can choose to reach out to the world again. I've found in my solitude that I greatly desire fellowship with others. It is my aloneness that has given me this gift.

I accept the lessons of aloneness
that help me find myself.

— ❀ —

. . no one who learns to know himself
remains just what he was before.
– Thomas Mann

I Am Finding Myself

Each day, though feeling pain, I learn more about who I've been and who I am becoming.

As I understand more about how my attachment ended, I am surprised at my humanity. My love has enabled me to show my tenderness. My sorrow has revealed my ability to feel empathy and compassion. My anger has given me energy and strength. Uncovering these things helps me tap into a deeper self than I knew before. This discovery gives me hope and courage to continue learning.

I am finding myself and this is wonderful.

Today, I dwell on what I've learned about myself.
I rejoice in my own growth.

– ❄ –

It is impossible to outperform your self-image.
— Earnie Larsen

I Am Who I See

My life is filled with many people, places, and events. In my experiences with them recently, I now see that I've been focusing on the dark side rather than the light, on defeat rather than success. This leaves me feeling all the more empty.

I've dwelt so long on my failures that this dark outlook has become comfortable. I give too much attention to my short-comings and quickly reject my virtues. Then I withdraw and remain fearful of making more mistakes. How will I ever be happy if I only notice negatives?

I will take this time to recognize my value and open myself to the world in ways I never have before. This is how I will create a positive self-image, a new vision of my life.

I see the bright side for a change. I am open to my goodness and my strengths.

— ❋ —

*If you do what you've always done, you'll get
what you've always gotten.*
– Unknown

When I Feel Guilt

As I remember my life with my loved one, I find many instances where I made mistakes: I acted in anger, I manipulated, I cried insincere tears, I was not always honest. By dwelling on these memories, I feel much guilt for what went wrong and really make myself suffer.

Now, I stand at a crossroads. I can follow the path of my guilt toward unhappiness, or I can take a different course and learn from my past behavior. I cannot change the past, but I can understand that following a pathway of guilt impedes my progress.

I did the best I could; rarely were my motives malicious. Let me dedicate my energy to new actions rather than old regrets. Life is too brief to mortgage it to the past. The present holds new promise.

*I see my past with understanding and
learn powerful lessons.*

– ❄ –

The quieter you become the more you can hear.
– Baba Ram Dass

I Will Know Myself

I am tired of the demands of others that steal my attention, my time, and my life. In the past I've sought to soothe myself through a barrage of activities, but these actions only pulled me further away from the peace within. So today, when I feel drained by outer circumstances, I will stop and reflect upon who I am.

I find that what I do is only a part of who I am. As I turn away from outside distractions, I hear the quiet voice of a deeper, more serene self.

What do I think? What do I feel? Where do I want to go? Let me consider my feelings, wants, and needs. As I listen, I will know myself and be renewed, to once again be a part of the world.

I will find my essence and learn that what I do must reflect this deeper self.

*I listen to my inner voice and
use its wisdom in life.*

– ❀ –

*Genuine beginnings begin within us,
even when they are brought to our attention
by external opportunities.*

– William Bridges

I Make Progress in Who I Am

Often, I seek to find my worth in my accomplishments. But presently it is difficult to find any satisfaction in them, so I believe what I've done and who I am are not worth very much. My pain has changed my perception of myself.

Instead of feeling like a failure, let me experience my changed life as a ripening process much like that of wine or cheese, in which the quality improves because of ingredients and time.

My goal in life is not perfection, but to keep developing myself. Because of continuing opportunities to grow and improve, I ripen with each passing day.

*Today, I view my loss as an opportunity
to improve myself.*

– ❋ –

That we are is God's gift to us.
Who we become is our gift to God.
– Unknown

What Can I Do?

One emotion that frustrates me more than any other is the feeling of powerlessness. I feel helpless when I watch how others' actions lead to grief, anger, fear, and despair. When my relationship ended, I came face to face with being powerless as I tried to persuade my partner to be what I desired. So I ask myself, "What can *I* do?"

The greatest task in life, the one I was born to handle, is dealing with myself. Much of my current anguish is prolonged by my unwillingness to be responsible for myself. Managing myself does not mean using willpower to control or stifle. Rather, it means making an effort to understand and experience all that I am. Being responsible for myself is having the courage to use what I've learned as I travel into the future with love, acceptance, and wisdom.

I accept my powerlessness over others.
I look within and understand my power
to influence myself.

– ❅ –

We cannot solve life's problems except
by solving them.
– M. Scott Peck

I Will Try, No, I Will Do It!

I was committed to my relationship. It ended and I fear that this may happen again. That fear prompts me to decide that from now on I won't ever become involved in a relationship, because I'm afraid it may fail. I know this attitude won't get me anywhere, but I find it difficult to try again.

Maybe that's the problem: All I've done is "try." I take on those activities or behaviors that appeal to me and avoid those that seem too difficult or painful. Perhaps my current troubles don't result from what I've done, but from what I haven't done. Or, maybe I'm in this situation because I've only lived life halfway instead of giving it my full effort.

My loss is beyond my control, but how I respond to it is up to me. Regardless of others' behavior, I can choose my actions.

What I *do* during this time points me toward who I will *be* in the future.

*Today, I do what needs to be done.
I fulfill my commitment to myself.*

— ❋ —

When you know you are doing your very best
within the circumstances of your existence,
applaud yourself!
– Rusty Berkus

The Tyranny in Today

How many times have I felt a "tyranny"
in today? How often have I thought, *Today,*
I must solve all my problems? Today, I have
to re-form the scattered pieces of my life.
Today, I will chart the best future, one far
different from my past. It isn't present
events, but hauntings of the past and
tauntings of the future that place so much
stress on me.

To go through this day for what it is, not
as other days have been lived, releases me
from this pressure. For today is *this* precious twenty-four hours of light and dark,
sounds and silence. The past is gone. All
my tomorrows are only as shadows seen
through half-opened eyes.

I can handle this twenty-four hour
period. As I do the best I possibly can,
I start to build from this day forward.

*I release my thoughts of the past and hold back
my fantasies for the future. I am simply here,
in this place, at this time.*

— ❄ —

I'm always ready to learn, although I do not always like being taught.
— Winston Churchill

The Lessons of Leftovers

Even as I heal, I'm reminded that I still hurt. I'm suddenly drawn back into that old pain, flooded by those familiar feelings. It seems to happen when I'm least prepared: While I look at forgotten photographs, when a friend casually shares information about my former partner, or simply when I hear a certain song on the radio. These reminders are my leftovers.

Yet, there are lessons in these leftovers. These remaining feelings show me where I still need to heal. They also remind me that I no longer endure this pain continually. I don't suffer as much now as I did then, it doesn't last long, and it isn't nearly as intense. And since I'm more willing and able to feel my emotions, I now work through unfinished issues without denial.

Experiencing leftovers is not easy. Like my loss, old feelings and memories occur without my permission. But, they are my teachers. From them I learn just where I am in my recovery.

I learn from leftovers what I've accomplished as well as what remains to be done.
I celebrate my growth.

— ❋ —

*Friend: One who knows all about you
and loves you just the same.*
– Elbert Hubbard

The Warmth of Friendship

With my love gone, this life seems flat, colorless, empty of all I hold dear. Seeing other people continue on as if nothing has happened only magnifies my pain. So, I mumble vague pleasantries and avoid all meaningful contact with others. I miss having friendship, the best part of my love-relationship. Though that is gone, I still desire this companionship with another.

There are those who ask me how I am and really seem sincere. They were friends before, and though they've seen me isolate myself, they still reach out to me. Perhaps they will listen to my sadness and genuinely understand. Surely some of them have had a similar ordeal.

I'll reach out to people who care about me. I'll take my memories of friendship and create new bonds, for there's much warmth left in me to share with others.

Today, I seek the warmth of friends. I break my shell of isolation and find companionship.

– ❄ –

We must all hang together or
we will hang separately.
– Ben Franklin

Healing Together

I've learned that loss creates space for something new. Though I often feel alone, I know I'm not. Others around me have experienced similar losses. We share a silent kinship that gives us the opportunity to build new bonds with each other.

I can share my emptiness and hurt by confiding in others who have experienced a loss. My unhappiness was created by the ending of a relationship. Building new, healthy friendships may be the best way to help me heal and become a healing force for others.

As I work to restore myself, I will share my process. Together we can reveal our unhappiness, free our anger, and let go of fear. United we can do what we cannot do alone: Heal from our loss by finding life again.

I help myself and others as I share
my healing process.

— ❄ —

To see a world in a grain of sand,
And heaven in a wildflower.
Hold infinity in the palm of your hand,
An eternity in an hour.
– William Blake

I Am in Tune With Life

This day I will be still, listen, and see what is around me. I will hear the beating of my heart. I will see wind move the leaves on trees and notice the lazy looks of pets as they simply exist. I will remain quiet and feel my life as part of all life within the harmony of nature.

All that has raged and been broken within me will be comforted as I appreciate the rhythms in nature's simple order. I breathe, I eat, and I live on. I realize that no matter what happens to me, these bonds with the rest of the natural world are unbreakable. Being in tune with nature helps me rejoice again in who I am.

Today, I quiet my inner turmoil and perceive
what is around me. I see my place in nature
and am refreshed.

– ❄ –

What we call the beginning is often an end.
And to make an end is to make a beginning.
The end is where we start from.

– T. S. Eliot

Letting Go

At times I feel as if I'm dangling from a narrow ledge, and my fingers ache from the effort. I can hardly grasp this ledge, the world I knew before my loss.

I fear letting go because I believe I'll fall into a nothingness that may last forever. What has been is over, what is now is painful, and what will be appears so uncertain. Yet, as my future rapidly approaches, I feel an exciting and sometimes terrifying urge to let go and separate myself from my past.

As I do let go, I find it is not me that falls, but my former life that falls away from me. I am set free with a new sense of myself and my world where I believe a better future will be mine. I am aware of my strength to find a new life.

I let go of my loss and greet this day with a sense of newness. I do not forget, but I do not live in the past. I simply go on.

– ❄ –

We meet to celebrate.
– Paula Reingold

I Celebrate My New Life

This experience has altered my identity, so much that I sometimes wonder who I am. In the past, my security and wholeness was woven into my relationship. This loss has changed that. Now, I am different.

I've had to let go of the past, both the good and the bad. And while this change brings some confusion, I've become clear about one thing: This transition gives me the opportunity to learn more about myself. I can be a better companion and friend to myself than I've ever been. The idea of being my own best friend pleases me. While I may not always have other people in my life, I'll have myself forever!

Today, I look kindly at myself.
As I celebrate a new life, I learn who I am.

– ❄ –

No man is an island.
— John Donne

We Are a Community

Though people with houses on the real estate market discover other "For Sale" signs everywhere, I seem to see only those most unlike me – happy couples sharing their joy. Doing this often perpetuates my loneliness, because it reminds me of my loss rather than my connections to others.

But noticing others together reminds me that we are a community of people. Though I may envy those couples, I don't know what difficulties they overcame to enjoy their present state. And who can foresee the happiness my own future holds?

We are all members of a larger community. I can reach out to this community and share my pain as well as my other emotions. As I do this, I know I am not alone.

I am part of all humankind, the greater whole of life. I draw energy from this community to help me heal.

— ❄ —

They knew they were pilgrims. . . so they committed themselves to the will of God and resolved to proceed.
– William Bradford

I Can Believe in Me

I want to find someone I can trust, but this is difficult. For too long I trusted a relationship that did not last. Who can I trust now?

Seeking trust is like looking for love. It's the search for something that's found not outside myself, but within me. I've often pursued a person, group, or ideal hoping I would regain trust. Yet, without trust in my own judgment, I will never be able to trust others.

I need to stop looking outside myself and, with the help of my Higher Power, begin to trust myself. I can start in small ways: Keeping promises to myself about healthy habits like diet, exercise, and time for fun; fulfilling commitments; and doing other things that are important to me. I can take time to be with people who nourish me, and reserve space for solitude, meditation, and spiritual growth. Soon, trust in myself will grow. When I find this trust, it follows that I will be able to trust others.

I trust myself and thereby find I can trust others. I realize my worthiness and, like the pilgrims, have a new, worthwhile life.

— ❈ —

We all carry it within us: supreme strength, the fullness of wisdom, unquenchable joy. It is never thwarted and cannot be destroyed.

– Huston Smith

The Foundation of My Being

This time of pain has stripped away the surface of my life and forced me to dig into myself. As I delved deeper, I not only found the energy to survive, I discovered my foundation.

This foundation of my being is the bedrock upon which I stand. It is made of my connection to my Higher Power and provides the will not just to live, but to thrive. In this place, I know I am a worthwhile person and that I have the power to heal.

Though I'll experience other losses and times of sorrow, anger, and fear, I will remain consciously connected to my deepest self. This is where I come home to my innate goodness and ability to restore myself.

Today, I acknowledge the goodness and power of my being. I build my new life on this foundation.

– ❄ –

*I was always complaining about the ruts in the
road until I realized that the ruts are the road.*
— A Twelve Step program recovery saying

Life Is Difficult

I've spent much energy looking for an
easier way through my present difficulties.
Yet, I always find there's no alternative to
understanding how this loss has changed
my life and working through my feelings
about it. Though difficult, this healing work
is quite rewarding.

As I strive to get beyond this painful
time, it's important not to fool myself. This
ordeal will end while the ordinary difficulties of living will not. I cannot know the
future. All I can bring with me are the
lessons of my past. I will learn them well
because I know the future will test me.

Life is difficult, but I am strong. I trust
my ability to work problems through,
rather than waste energy looking for an
easier way.

*I accept life and all it teaches me.
Each day I learn more about living and healing.*

— ❄ —

*Energy is the power that drives every
human being. It is not lost by exertion
but maintained by it.*
— Germaine Greer

I'll Feel Like It When I Do It

I know I should get on with my life, but
there are times when I feel like I'm on
"empty," stagnant, and have no energy at
all. While most of my pain and anger are
gone, this strange emptiness remains. I
don't hurt. I don't feel much of anything.
Even the thought of moving into the world
drains me.

So I sit and wonder at what the world
may do to me next while I watch for
opportunities and wait for a spark to ignite
me back to life. I should do something, but
I've been waiting until I felt like it. Now,
more than ever, my immobility is holding
me back. It is time for me to make the effort
to go into the world instead of waiting for
it to come to me. As I act, my momentum
builds energy. I begin to feel new power to
help me risk again. So instead of waiting

until I feel like it, I'll feel like it when I do it.
What a new lesson in living I've learned!

Today, I put energy into living.

— ❄ —

They can because they think they can.
– Virgil

I Will Hide No More

For too long I've hidden behind my facade of grief and anger. To be sure, much of it has been honest anguish. Yet, now what I am showing to others and myself is not really pain; it is a mask to keep me from taking risks.

I will outgrow my mourning self and open the curtains of my life once again, and let the sun shine on the newness of who I've become. I will no longer hide from challenges. There is so much to do, to be. I find that pain has changed to excitement as life returns and I am so eager to live as my new self.

I am myself as I let go of the security of pain.
I replace my fear with the excitement of a new life.

– ❋ –

A man can only be young once, but he can be immature forever.
– Catherine Aird

Growing Old, Getting Smart

There have been periods in my life when I thought I had it made. A successful career, happy family, and rewarding pursuits added to my self-congratulation. I had problems then also, but I handled them with self-confidence and wisdom. Then I lost my relationship. I've come to realize that my part in the loss was the damage I caused when I acted unwisely, behaved foolishly, and at times was unashamedly selfish.

Now I understand that maturity doesn't naturally arrive with age. This insight may be the most mature I've had so far. If I am to grow wiser as I grow older, I must confront my shortcomings and humbly identify and accept my faults as I practice new thoughts and behavior.

The joys of living are all too short. As a human being I know I'll make more mistakes in my life. I will do my best to make them new ones!

I accept responsibility for my shortcomings and am more able to express myself with humility.

– ❄ –

God don't make no junk.

– A Twelve Step program recovery saying

The Goodness from My Guilt

In my relationship, I often behaved in ways I now regret – acts of selfishness, emotional outbursts, demands for attention, attempts to control. Though I recognize my human limitations, these behaviors leave me with guilt. How can I atone for these actions?

What was will never be again. I cannot go back and relive my life a different way. Learning from the past will help me live better in the future, but it will not make up for what I did wrong. This can only be accomplished when I make amends.

I'll share the substance of these actions along with my regrets. I do this first with a trusted friend. Then, if I can, I'll speak with the person I've harmed. I'll take responsibility for my behavior, share my feelings of remorse, and ask for forgiveness from that person as well as from myself. Finally making amends means I will change those behaviors that cause such hurt. Doing this will give me the measure of peace I seek, for then I can release my guilt and with it let go of those painful memories of the past.

Today, I celebrate my humanness and free myself from guilt.

– ❄ –

*A journey of a thousand miles must begin
with a single step.*
– Lao-tzu

Now I Understand

After all this time, I understand what happened. I finally see the reasons for my pain. I'm aware of what my relationship was and why it ended. It seems so easy now to go forward with my new knowledge and create happiness with one bold stroke. But understanding is not doing, and insight alone is not change.

I *have* changed; the new me stands ready to confront the complexities of the world. But my hard-won wisdom must be tested carefully within the risks of real life. While I'm joyful with my new energy and willingness, I must temper this feeling by remembering that I had a similar confidence before my loss.

Let me understand the improvements in myself. I'll be sensible but not timid, for though I've learned much, there's more to discover.

*I use the lessons of my loss to guide me
back into the world.*

– ❀ –

Experience is not what happens to a man. It is what a man does with what happens to him.
– Aldous Huxley

The Scars on My Heart

There is no doubt that I have changed. So far, what I've done to cope has stopped the emotional pain and helped me bind up my wounds. But, scars remain, and they affect me through the fear I have of approaching others.

As if armored against the possibility of repeating the past, I hold back from others – walled, protected, and wary. I remember all too well how painful severed relationships can be.

The scars on my heart are from this past pain, and they tell of my experience. My scars remind me to be wary, but not to withhold myself completely. While I don't want more pain, I also don't want to be alone. So, I will take the risk to share my heart again, scars and all.

Today, I release my fear and risk sharing myself with others again.

– ❀ –

. . . he who finds himself loses his misery.
– Matthew Arnold

Who Is That in My Mirror?

I see someone in the mirror, and I know it's not me. Who is it then? Who is that person with the soft smile and glowing eyes? There must be some mistake.

For too long, my mirror has shown me a haggard face pulled down by the weight of loss. But now I look into the glass and wonder who that is. This person looks alive, happy, excited, full of energy. Could it be that I've changed? Could this person be me?

I know I'm becoming different as I heal, but I never realized how different. I've become so accustomed to being miserable that it will take work to accept a happier me. What fun this will be!

I accept happiness into my life.
I am worthy of joy.

– ❋ –

Every individual is an expression of the whole realm of nature, a unique action of the total universe.

– Alan Watts

Exploring Singleness

One constant fact throughout this time is that I've always had myself. Oh, I didn't always want to be with me. There were many times when I avoided my mirror, got lost in someone else's problems, made myself so busy I left no time to consider my inner world. When I finally stopped and looked, I saw a person sad, angry, lonely, or afraid. I didn't like myself then. Now, as I'm working through my loss, I realize I'm different. And, I'm still here.

Regardless of my wishes for a lasting love-relationship, there are no guarantees. If there's one connection I'm certain of, though, it's the one with myself. Regardless of my relationship status, I'll always be an individual, a single human being. Knowing this gives me a new direction.

I must explore this individuality. I need to know the depth of my feelings, the breadth of my thoughts. I must honor my uniqueness and know that my needs and desires are worthy.

I celebrate myself in exploring my individuality.

— ❋

Life has got to be lived – that's all there is to it.
At 70 I would say the advantage is that you
take life more calmly. You know that
"This, too, shall pass."

– Eleanor Roosevelt

I Am Moving On

Time passes. I know that some day all
my experiences will be memories. I have
lived through this loss and it too is passing
from me. I am moving on.

I am not so naive as to believe all my
problems are solved just because this storm
is over. Wisely, I'll remember that future
experiences will bring back painful
thoughts and feelings. I do understand,
though, that a major struggle has ended,
and I am stronger because of it.

I feel the stirrings of something pro-
found, something central to my life, all life.
I sense the beginnings of love. Like the
smallest green tendril winding toward the
sun, my love grows. It is love for myself
and for the opportunity of life. I know
this love will blossom someday into the

willingness to be vulnerable again. I'm not ready for that yet, but it will come.

Today, I sense my life has been renewed.
I enter it with joy and love.

— ❄ —

Some men see the way things are and ask,
"Why?" I see things that never were
and ask, "Why not?"
– Robert F. Kennedy

AFTERWORD
A New Beginning

Nothing lasts forever. With change as our constant companion, we cannot avoid losses. We can only get better at accepting them and learning from our experience.

The loss of a love-relationship is a crisis. Though painful, this suffering has a beginning, a middle, and an end. We can choose to live through it and beyond into the future.

The pain of our loss will remain a permanent part of who we are. We will not forget it, just as we will not forget the relationship we've mourned. There is no doubt we have learned much. Through the power of healing, we find new awareness.

We have been in pain and now we are beginning again, renewed and more than we were before. This beginning is different. We have new wisdom won from facing life as it is, not as we might have desired it. To be grounded in reality gives us real strength to improve the life we have.

As we complete our journey through this loss, we gain a greater love for our Higher Power and for all of life. And this will lead us to love again.

— ❄ —

Index